D1588152

Princess Margaret
1930 – 2002

Antony,
Earl of Snowdon
b. 1930
(divorced 1978)

David,
Viscount Linley
b. 1961

Serena
Stanhope
b. 1970

Lady Sarah
Armstrong-Jones
b. 1964

Daniel
Chatto
b. 1957

Charles
Armstrong-Jones
b. 1999

Margarita
Armstrong-Jones
b. 2002

Samuel
Chatto
b. 1996

Arthur
Chatto
b. 1999

ndrew,
e of York
. 1960

Sarah Ferguson
b. 1959
(divorced 1996)

Edward,
Earl of Wessex
b. 1964

Sophie
Rhys-Jones
b. 1965

eatrice,
ess of York
. 1988

Eugenie,
Princess of York
b. 1990

Lady
Louise Windsor
b. 2003

James,
Viscount Severn
b. 2007

LADYBIRD BOOKS

UK | USA | Canada | Ireland | Australia
India | New Zealand | South Africa

Ladybird Books is part of the Penguin Random House group of companies whose addresses
can be found at global.penguinrandomhouse.com.

ladybird.com

First published 2016
Some content in this book was previously published in *HM Queen Elizabeth II: Diamond Jubilee*
001

Copyright © Ladybird Books Ltd, 2016
Written by Fiona Munro.
The moral right of the author has been asserted.

Printed in China

A CIP catalogue record for this book is available from the British Library

ISBN: 978-0-241-24032-8

Picture Credits

The publisher would like to thank the following for their kind permission to reproduce their photographs:
Jacket (front l) Corbis / Bettmann; Jacket (front r) Getty Images / UK Press / Pool / Mark Cuthbert; Jacket (back) Getty Images
AFP / Ian McIlgorm; 5 Getty Images / AFP / Ian McIlgorm; 6bl Corbis / Hulton-Deutsch Collection; 6cra Getty Images / Centr
Press; 7tl Getty Images / Universal History Archive; 7b Getty Images / Lisa Sheridan / Studio Lisa; 8tl Getty Images / Universa
History Archive; 8br Corbis / Bettmann; 9 Corbis / Bettmann; 10 Getty Images / Bert Hardy / Picture Post / Hulton Archive;
11 Getty Images / Rolls Press / Popperfoto; 12tr Photoshot / UPPA; 12bl (Paris Vue) Getty Images / Apic; 12fbl (Picture Post)
Getty Images / Picture Post / IPC Magazines / Hulton Archive; 13t Corbis / David Boyer / National Geographic Creative; 13b
Getty Images / Hulton Archive; 14tl Corbis / Bettmann; 14b Corbis / Bettmann; 15t Getty Images / Keystone; 15br Getty Imag
/ Hulton Archive; 16cra Getty Images / Keystone; 16b Getty Images / Popperfoto; 17t Press Association Images / PA Archive /
Steve Parsons; 17br Press Association Images / PA Archive / Fiona Hanson; 18b Getty Images / WPA Pool / Anthony Devlin;
19tr Getty Images / Popperfoto / Rolls Press; 19b Getty Images / AFP / John Stillwell; 20b Getty Images / Sion Touhig; 21t Get
Images / Chris Jackson; 21br Corbis / Albert Nieboer / dpa; 22 GettyImages / AFP/ David Bebber; 23t Getty Images / Rota / Anw
Hussein; 23b Getty Images / Ullstein Bild / Camera 4 Fotoagentur; 24tr Getty Images / Spencer Arnold/ Alexander Bassano; 24
Getty Images / Rota / WireImage/ Anwar Hussein Collection; 25 Getty Images / WPA Pool / Chris Jackson; 26tr Getty Images
Indigo/ Max Mumby; 26b Getty Images / PA Wire / The Duke and Duchess of Cambridge; 27 Getty Images / WireImage/ Anw
Hussein; 28tr Corbis / Bettmann; 29 Getty Images / UK Press / Pool / Mark Cuthbert
(Abbreviations key: a-above; b-below/bottom; c-centre; f-far; l-left; r-right; t-top)

A LADYBIRD SOUVENIR

HM QUEEN ELIZABETH II

*90*TH BIRTHDAY CELEBRATION

A Royal Baby is Born

When Elizabeth was born into the Royal Family, she was never expected to one day be Queen.
She was third in line to the throne behind her uncle, Edward, Prince of Wales, and her father.

Elizabeth was born in London at 2:40 a.m. on 21 April 1926, the first child of the Duke and Duchess of York. She was given the names Elizabeth Alexandra Mary.

A baby Princess Elizabeth with her parents

Elizabeth as a child

Her first name was after her mother, the second after her great-grandmother, Queen Alexandra, and the third after her grandmother, Queen Mary.

When Elizabeth was four, her sister, Margaret Rose, was born. The family were very close and spent many happy times together, often at Royal Lodge, their new home in Windsor Great Park.

Elizabeth and her little sister, Margaret

The family in the grounds at Windsor Castle, 1936

A NEW ROLE
FOR THE FAMILY

Elizabeth playing as a child

Princess Elizabeth or 'Lilibet', as she called herself, enjoyed a carefree childhood until she was ten, when her life was turned upside down. In January 1936, her grandfather King George V died and was succeeded by her uncle who was crowned Edward VIII. He had reigned less than a year when he stepped down from the throne in order to marry an American divorcee. In 1936 it was impossible for the king to marry a divorced woman, and Edward was determined to be with Wallis Simpson. The crown passed to Elizabeth's father, who was crowned King George VI just before Christmas in 1936.

Elizabeth was now heir to the throne

With their father as King, the young princesses had to get used to life in the spotlight. For the young Elizabeth, the unexpected change in royal succession would have enormous consequences. It meant that one day she would be Queen.

The coronation of King George VI

A ROYAL WEDDING

The royal bride and groom

In 1939, when Elizabeth was thirteen years old, the Second World War broke out. The young princess was keen to help and, in early 1945, aged nineteen, she joined the Auxiliary Territorial Service (ATS). This was the women's branch of the Army. Elizabeth worked as a volunteer and by the end of the war, in 1945, she was a Junior Commander and a qualified driver!

In 1939, Elizabeth also met her future husband, Prince Philip of Greece. He was an officer in the Royal Navy. The couple kept in touch by letter during the war, and were married at Westminster Abbey in November 1947. It was a simple occasion, as the country was still recovering from wartime restrictions. Elizabeth collected clothing coupons for her dress, just like any other bride. Coming after such a time of sadness, the excitement of a royal wedding was welcomed by people all around the world.

The happy couple pose for photographs on their wedding day

A Crowning Moment

On 6 February 1952, when Princess Elizabeth and Philip were mid-way through a global tour, they were told the sad news of her father's death.

The tour was abandoned, and the young princess, aged just twenty-five, flew back to England as Queen. The coronation of Queen Elizabeth II took place at Westminster Abbey on 2 June 1953. It was a spectacular event, and Elizabeth took her vows with great dignity. Crowds lined the streets to catch a glimpse of their new Queen. The ceremony was broadcast on the radio and the coronation was the first major international event to be aired on television. Three-quarters of the people in Britain watched the broadcast, and for many, it was the first time they had ever seen a television.

The coronation was reported around the world

Thousands of people stood along the procession route

Of Queen Elizabeth's children, only Prince Charles and Princess Anne had been born by the time of the coronation. They joined their mother on the balcony of Buckingham Palace after the ceremony, just as Elizabeth and Margaret had joined their parents after King George VI's coronation.

The Royal Family on the balcony of Buckingham Palace

A NEW ROYAL FAMILY

Elizabeth's first child, Prince Charles, was born at Buckingham Palace in 1948, before she became Queen. Shops closed and people celebrated up and down the country. Then, in 1950, he was followed by a sister, Princess Anne. A second son, Prince Andrew, was born in 1960 and her fourth child, Prince Edward, was born in 1964.

Prince Charles as a baby

Prince Charles and his sister, Princess Anne, with their parents

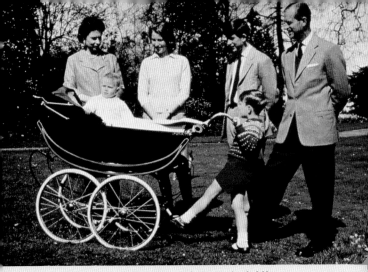

Prince Edward, born in 1964, was the Queen's fourth child

When it was time to educate their children, Queen Elizabeth and Prince Philip broke with tradition by being the first members of the Royal Family to send their children to school. Elizabeth, by contrast, had been educated at home by governesses, and perhaps realized that the rough and tumble of the playground was a better introduction to the world for her children.

Prince Charles (far left)
at prep school with friends, 1957

A ROYAL LIFE

As Head of State, the Queen had many new duties to perform. There were documents to read and sign, important ceremonies to attend and regular meetings with the Prime Minister.

The Queen reading documents at her desk in Buckingham Palace

The Queen delivers her first Christmas speech from Sandringham House, 1952

The Queen talking to a young well-wisher

Over the years, Her Royal Highness, often with Prince Philip at her side, has visited more than 120 different countries around the world. She always seems perfectly comfortable, whether addressing a crowd of thousands, or crouching to listen to the whispered words of a small child.

In 2014, the Queen undertook 393 royal engagements. That is more than one a day! Although she is soon approaching her ninetieth birthday, the Queen still plays a very important role in politics.

The Queen travels around the world meeting key dignitaries from many countries

THE QUEEN AROUND THE WORLD

Her Majesty the Queen is not just Head of State in the United Kingdom. She is also Sovereign of fifteen other Commonwealth countries: Australia, New Zealand, Canada, Jamaica, Antigua and Barbuda, the Bahamas, Barbados, Grenada, Belize, St Lucia, St Christopher and Nevis, the Solomon Islands, Tuvalu, St Vincent and the Grenadines, and Papua New Guinea, as well as Head of the Commonwealth itself.

The Queen helps to connect all of these diverse nations and promote friendship and negotiation. It cannot always be easy, and there is a great deal of protocol to remember, but the Queen instinctively knows both how to greet a child in Australia and chat to the King of Tonga.

Queen Elizabeth receives Queen Nanasipau'u and King George Tupou VI of Tonga at Buckingham Palace, 2013

In the United Kingdom, the Queen takes a caring interest in the state papers submitted to her each day and meets with the British Prime Minister every week. Although it is important that the

The Queen and Winston Churchill, 1955

Queen expresses no political views in public, this meeting is an opportunity for Her Majesty to express her thoughts on the current political situation and to ask questions on particular topics.

The Queen and Prime Minister David Cameron, 2011

IMPORTANT EVENTS

The Queen's incredible sixty-four years of almost non-stop official visits and state occasions have been punctuated by some key events. With her family, she has celebrated many happy times but, like most people, she has also suffered her fair share of sadness and tragedy.

Wonderful highlights for the Queen have been the marking of her Jubilees. The flags flew in 1977 to celebrate her Silver Jubilee. Then her Golden Jubilee and Diamond Jubilee were commemorated in 2002 and 2012 respectively. The three happy occasions were celebrated with special events and large-scale tours.

The Queen's Gold State Coach makes its way down the Mall during Her Majesty's Golden Jubilee celebrations, 2002

The newly married Duke and Duchess of Cambridge in Westminster Abbey

In April 2011, the Queen and the rest of the world rejoiced in the marriage of her grandson Prince William to Catherine Middleton. It was clear that the Queen enjoyed the day tremendously. This was followed by a much smaller – but by no means less enjoyable – wedding that summer that saw Her Majesty's eldest granddaughter, Zara Phillips, marry ex-England rugby player, Mike Tindall.

The Queen enjoys spending time with her family and it must have been wonderful to be able to share two extremely happy events with so many family members.

Mike and Zara Tindall
on their wedding day, 2011

A Glittering Jubilee

The Queen's Diamond Jubilee and the London Olympics marked a spectacular year for Her Majesty in 2012 and there were many events arranged to celebrate a very special time.

The Thames Diamond Jubilee Pageant took place on the River Thames and saw around 1,000 boats of every size and type from all across the world take part.

Madness performing on the roof of Buckingham Palace at the Diamond Jubilee Concert

Over 2,000 celebratory beacons were lit throughout the UK and Commonwealth and a host of famous faces performed in a concert that took place outside Buckingham Palace. These exciting events culminated with a carriage procession and a spectacular fireworks display.

Queen Elizabeth on the royal barge Gloriana

The Olympic Games, the first to take place in the United Kingdom since 1948, were a fitting ending to an incredible few months for Her Majesty. The breathtaking opening ceremony was watched by an estimated worldwide audience of 900 million people. It also showed the Queen's keen sense of humour. She had agreed to take part in a pre-recorded scene with Daniel Craig as James Bond, and had a stunt double who parachuted from a plane into the Olympic stadium. The cheers were deafening!

A stunt double jumps from a plane during the Olympic opening ceremony

Sixty Glorious Years

The Diamond Jubilee in 2012 celebrated sixty years of the Queen's reign. Only one other British monarch has ever achieved such a milestone, and that was Queen Victoria, who celebrated her Diamond Jubilee in 1897.

A portrait of Queen Victoria, 1882

When Elizabeth was crowned in 1952, the Second World War had not long ended and the world was very different. Rationing was still in place and the fir televisions had only just begun to appear for sale.

It is also astonishing to think that Her Royal Highness has given her regular weekly audience to twelve different Prime Ministers. When our currer Prime Minister, David Cameron, was born in 1966 she had already been on the throne for fourteen years!

Queen Elizabeth after delivering her Christmas message, 2008

Even though the Queen is gradually handing over some of her royal duties, she is still patron of more then 600 charities – over 400 of which she has held since her coronation.

The Queen has lived through ninety years of enormous social and technological change. On Her Majesty's twenty-first birthday she dedicated her life to the service of the Commonwealth. She said, 'My whole life whether it be long or short shall be devoted to your service'. In contrast to that crackly radio broadcast, the Queen's ninetieth birthday will be documented on the Royal Family website and the Royal Family Channel on YouTube. There will also be news on the royal Twitter, Facebook and Instagram accounts!

Queen Elizabeth and Prince Philip viewing the 'Blood Swept Lands and Seas of Red' installation at the Tower of London, 2014

THE NEXT GENERATION

The Queen is close to all her grandchildren, and shows obvious delight as each new great-grandchild comes along. The first child of the Duke and Duchess of Cambridge, George Alexander Louis – or Prince George of Cambridge – was born at 4:24 p.m. on 22 July 2013 to great excitement all over the world.

Zara Tindall with baby Mia Grace, who was born on 17 January 2014

Prince George of Cambridge at Kensington Palace, 2014

The Duke and Duchess of Cambridge with the newborn Princess Charlotte, 2015

Prince George was followed almost two years later, on 2 May 2015 at 8:24 a.m., by a sister. Charlotte Elizabeth Diana – Princess Charlotte of Cambridge – is a very special baby girl. Of course, every new baby is special and unique, but Princess Charlotte is the first female royal baby born into the immediate Royal Family since the rules of succession were changed. Since 1701, princes have taken precedence over their sisters but the new rules mean that Charlotte will remain fourth in line to the throne, even if her parents go on to have another son. Her birth also pushes her uncle, Prince Harry, down to fifth in line to the throne.

Happy Birthday, Your Majesty!

The Queen will be ninety years old on 21 April 2016. There will be many festivities to mark this special birthday – yet another significant moment in an already historic reign – but they will centre around a special series of shows celebrating the Queen's lifelong

Queen Elizabeth at her coronation, 1953

passion for horses. The event will feature 600 horses and 1,500 performers from around the world, and will pay tribute to many of the events that have been so important throughout her long life.

The Queen has guided her family and her subjects with calm dignity through good times and bad, and it is a job she has undertaken faultlessly, elegantly and with a warm smile. May she continue to do so for years to come.

Congratulations, Your Majesty, on your ninetieth birthday!

Queen Elizabeth II at the Presidential Palace in Lithuania, 2006